This poetry book belongs to

....

OXFORD
UNIVERSITY PRESS

Great Clarendon Street, Oxford OX2 6DP, United Kingdom

Oxford University Press is a department of the University of Oxford.
It furthers the University's objective of excellence in research,
scholarship, and education by publishing worldwide

Illustrations by: Marc Vyvyan-Jones, Graham Round, Elsa Houghton, Paul Dowling, Chris
Smedley, Jan Nesbitt, Jenny Williams, Renée Andriani, John Dyke, Tony Ross, Korky Paul,
Jane Gedye, Andy Cooke, Nick Sharratt, Alex Brychta, Peet Ellison, Phillippe Dupasquier,
Alan Marks, Caroline Jayne Church, Dominic Mansell, Jan Lewis, Anita Jeram, Diana
Mayo, Jo Burroughes

Cover illustration by: Nick Sharratt

British Library Cataloguing in Publication Data
Data available

978-0-19-274471-5

10 9 8 7 6 5 4 3 2 1

Printed in China

Paper used in the production of this book is a natural, recyclable product made
from wood grown in sustainable forests.The manufacturing process conforms to
the environmental regulations of the country of origin.

I Can Read! Oxford Poetry

For 6 Year Olds

With foreword by
Series Editor, John Foster

OXFORD

Acknowledgements

We are grateful to the authors in each case unless otherwise stated, for permission to include their poems:

Sue Cowling, 'Fast Food Giant', first published in *Giant Poems* (OUP, 1991), © Sue Cowling 1991.

Richard Edwards, 'Wizard' and 'The Wizard Said', first published in *Wizard Poems* (OUP, 1991), © Richard Edwards 1991.

Eric Finney, 'The Day the Hose Flipped', first published in *Water Poems* (OUP, 1993), © Eric Finney 1993, 'All Giants', first published in *Giant Poems* (OUP, 1991) and 'Just Practising', first published in *Wizard Poems* (OUP, 1991), © Eric Finney 1991, reprinted by permission of Mrs Sheilagh Finney.

John Foster, 'The Double-Decker Bus' and 'Driving Along', first published in *Transport Poems* (OUP, 1993), © John Foster 1993; 'On A Starry Night', first published in *Star Poems* (OUP, 1991) © John Foster 1991; 'Giant Griff', first published in *Giant Poems* (OUP, 1991) © John Foster 1991; and with John Rice: 'Instructions for Giants', © John Rice and John Foster 1991.

Richard James, 'I've Made a Machine' and 'The Time Machine', first published in *Machine Poems* (OUP, 1996), and 'Kitchen Sounds' first published in *Senses Poems* (OUP, 1996), © Richard Edwards 1995.

Jean Kenward, 'Ogre', first published in *Giant Poems* (OUP, 1991) © Jean Kenward 1991.

John Kitching, 'Magic Man', first published in *Wizard Poems* (OUP, 1991), © John Kitching 1991.

Wendy Larmont, 'Meddling Muddle', first published in *Wizard Poems* (OUP, 1991), © Wendy Larmont 1991.

Ian McMillan, 'Ten Things Found in a Wizard's Pocket', first published in *Wizard Poems* (OUP, 1991), reprinted by permission of UK Touring on behalf of the author.

Tony Mitton, 'Mr Mad's Machine', first published in *Transport Poems* (OUP, 1993), and 'Many Ways to Travel', first published in *Transport Poems* (OUP, 1993), © Tony Mitton 1993, reprinted by permission of David Higham Associates.

Brian Moses, 'Through the Dark' first published in *Night Poems* (OUP, 1991) and 'Moonbase Classroom Three', first published in *Space Poems* (OUP, 1991), © Brian Moses 1991.

Judith Nicholls, 'Giant Tale', first published in *Giant Poems* (OUP, 1991), © Judith Nicholls 1991.

Irene Rawnsley, 'The Giant Visitor', first published in *Giant Poems* (OUP, 1991) and 'Space Message', first published in *Space Poems* (OUP, 1991), © Irene Rawnsley 1991 reprinted by permission of Kate Rawnsley.

John Rice with John Foster, 'Instructions for Giants' first published in *Giant Poems* (OUP, 1991), © John Rice and John Foster 1991.

Marian Swinger, 'The Diggers', first published in *Machine Poems* (OUP, 1996), © Marian Swinger 1996.

Charles Thomson, 'Everything's Giant', first published in *Giant Poems* (OUP, 1991), and 'Spaceship Race', first published in *Space Poems* (OUP, 1991), © Charles Thomson 1991.

Celia Warren, 'Night Ride', first published in *Transport Poems* (OUP, 1993), © Celia Warren 1993, 2016.

Raymond Wilson, 'From a Space Rocket', first published in *Space Poems* (OUP, 1991), © Raymond Wilson 1991, reprinted by permission of Mrs G M Wilson.

Irene Yates, 'Journey into Space', first published in *Space Poems* (OUP, 1991), © Irene Yates 1991, and 'The Flying Reptile's Race', first published in *Sports Poems* (OUP 1990), © Irene Yates 1990.

Although we have made every effort to trace and contact all copyright holders before publication this has not been possible in all cases. If notified, the publisher will rectify any errors or omissions at the earliest opportunity.

Welcome!

This book provides a selection of poems to share with your child, which will help them become more confident with their reading. Children whose parents read with them at home and talk about what they read have a huge advantage at school.

The National Curriculum stresses the importance of children enjoying a variety of literary forms, not just stories. This includes an emphasis on reading and understanding poetry through learning, performing and reciting it. By Year 3 children should also be able to identify themes and express views.

When you read with your child, not only do they develop their reading skills, but they also learn that reading is a pleasurable activity. By reading and discussing poems together you can begin to foster an enjoyment of poetry that will extend beyond their schooldays.

As well as providing a lively collection of poems for you to share, this book contains practical tips on how to introduce the poems and suggestions for activities you can use after reading, such as how to prepare a performance.

I can remember sharing nursery rhymes and poems with my parents and with my own children. The shared experience of listening to and joining in with reciting poems is one of the reasons I started writing children's poetry. From an early age I developed an interest in the sound of words and how you could play with them to make up rhymes.

I have been lucky enough to be invited to put together collections of my own and other people's poems for you to share and enjoy with your child. I hope you will have as much fun reading and performing them together as I did choosing them.

John Foster

Contents

Sailing Past the Planets

Crashing Through the Ceiling

Enjoying poetry with your child

I Can Read! Oxford Poetry for 6 Year Olds is the second of three books which offer poems for parents to share and enjoy with their children. These poems are perfect for you and your child to read aloud together as they have strong **rhythms**, simple **rhyme schemes** and lots of repetition.

Poetry is ideal for younger readers. Often far shorter than a chapter of a book or short story, a poem allows a child to enter a fantastical world in just a page or two. This means that they may tackle several poems, or re-visit a poem many times, because they can access them quickly and easily. You can also use them as a way of introducing simple literary language, using terms such as **verse**, **rhythm** and **rhyme**. The glossary at the end of the book will help you to explain these terms to your child, which appear in pink throughout these notes.

Poetry is great for children's reading development and is a key part of the National Curriculum. This collection can be used either on its own or alongside storybooks such as the *Read with Biff, Chip and Kipper* series to develop reading skills and enjoyment. You can simply read and enjoy the poems in this book together, or use the notes and tips to help prepare your child to meet the National Curriculum requirements for poetry, which aim to develop children's ability to:

✓	Learn, recite and perform poems
✓	Listen to, read and discuss a wide range of poems
✓	Recognise simple literary language and use terms such as **verse**, **rhythm** and **rhyme**
✓	Show an understanding of poems while reading aloud through **intonation**, volume and action.

Tips and ideas for developing reading skills

Introducing literary language

★ Discuss words that sound similar to what they describe, known as **onomatopoeia**, and then read **Kitchen Sounds** (p. 16). Ask your child which words they think best echo the sound they describe. Ask your child to read the poem aloud, **emphasising** the sound words and bringing out the contrast between the kitchen during the day and the kitchen at night.

★ Read **The Diggers** (p. 20) and then ask your child what the poet compares the diggers to. Encourage them to pick out all the words and phrases, such as 'metal teeth', that suggest the diggers are biting into the earth like dinosaurs. Point out the **rhymes** in the poem and discuss how there is a **rhyme** in the middle of two lines which is separated by a number of other lines – 'prowl' and 'growl'. Talk about how the poem conveys the strength and power of the diggers and invite your child to try to express this when reading the poem.

★ Explain that a poem that tells a story is known as a **narrative** poem. Before reading **Through the Dark** (p. 34), point out how it is like a story. Discuss the way the child and Dad both speak in the poem and ask your child who they think the **narrator** is.

★ Encourage your child to learn and recite **The Time Machine** (p. 38). Point out how the poem is written in pairs of lines which **rhyme**, known as **couplets**, which give the poem a strong **rhythm**. Encourage them to recite the poem, perhaps varying their voice to sound like someone trying to sell the ride in the first **verse** then building to a dramatic climax in the last **verse**.

TOP TIP! Read the other poems in *Toasters Clang and Kettles Whistle* together and encourage your child to use some of the literary language introduced above and in the glossary when talking about them.

Recognising rhyme and rhythm

★ Read **Just Practising** (p. 44) together and talk about what happens in the poem. Point out how the poem is written in **couplets**, which give the poem a strong **rhythm**. Work together to think about what other things the wizard might have made appear and try to make up another **couplet** to add to the poem.

★ Read **Magic Man** (p. 52) and point out that it is a poem with a strong **rhythm** because it repeats the word 'magic'. Ask what else gives it a strong **rhythm**. How is it similar to **Just Practising**? Try performing it together to **emphasise** this **rhythm**, with both of you chanting the first eight lines and your child chanting the last two lines alone.

★ Share **Meddling Muddle** (p. 48) with your child and talk about what happens to the apprentice. Look at the use of speech marks and ask your child how a reader can tell who is saying what. Then decide who is going to read the different parts. Discuss the **verses** in which the wizard speaks and how his **tone** of voice would be different in each — commanding in the first **verse**, angry in the sixth **verse** and cold in the final **verse**.

TOP TIP! Ask your child to find some other poems in the book that have **couplets** or speech marks. Pick your favourite rhyming poem together and think up some extra lines or a new **verse**.

Discussing and comparing poems

★ Read **Space** (p. 54) and point out that the poem takes the form of a list with a humorous postscript at the end. Discuss the list of features of space that it mentions and encourage your child to suggest other features that the poet could have included. Write another **couplet** with your child to add to the poem, for example 'Astronauts and satellites / Bug-eyed aliens, meteorites.'

★ Share **Spaceship Race** (p. 60) together, then look at the illustration and discuss whether it helps you to understand the poem. Talk about what happens in the race and encourage your child to read it again. Discuss how reading it at a fast pace, **emphasising** words such as 'whizz' and 'whoosh', can capture the speed and drama of the action. Discuss how 'whoosh' is an example of **onomatopoeia** and find some more poems that use this device.

★ Talk about what the world looks like from space and then read **From a Space Rocket** (p. 70). Discuss what the message of the poem is and encourage them to read the poem in a way that conveys its message.

★ Draw attention to the fact that **Space**, **Moonbase Classroom Three** (p. 58) and **Spaceship Race** are light-hearted while **Space Message** (p. 66) and **From a Space Rocket** are serious poems. Ask your child which poems they prefer and encourage them to explain why.

TOP TIP! Pick one of the other sections of poems to read through and discuss the **themes** in the poems. Discuss the similarities and differences between poems with similar **themes**.

Performing poems

★ Share **Instructions for Giants** (p. 72) together. Talk about how you would ask a giant for something, then read the first **verse** in a pleading **tone**. Point out the **pattern** and **rhyme scheme** of the poem, and help your child to prepare a performance of the poem.

★ Read **Fast Food Giant** (p. 78) with your child. Ensure they understand what a **narrator** is and ask your child who that is in this poem, and how they can tell. Ask how we know that the giant is still hungry after eating the meal. Point out how the poem is written as an order in a fast food restaurant. Encourage your child to suggest ways of reading the poem to show the difference between Jack speaking and the giant speaking. Then try to perform the poem.

★ Read **All Giants** (p. 89) together. Discuss why it is called **All Giants**. Look at the use of speech marks and ask your child how they can tell who is saying what. Then decide who is going to read the different parts. Encourage your child to think about how the insects would speak – the ant in a tiny voice, perhaps? Maybe the butterfly would speak in a whispery voice and the bee in a buzzy voice? Practise performing the poem with one of you acting as **narrator** and the other as the insects.

TOP TIP! Encourage your child to learn poems off by heart and to perform and recite them. Let them choose their favourite poem from *Crashing Through the Ceiling* and help them to memorise it, then use actions and **intonation** to create a performance.

Toasters Clang
and
kettles Whistle

*Use a poem in this collection as a model and work together with your child to draft a similar poem. For example, you could draft your own poem called, 'My Mad Machine', which may be similar to **Mr Mad's Machine**. Dictionaries like the **Oxford First Rhyming Dictionary** may be useful to help you find* rhymes.

I've Made a Machine

I've made a machine
That can fly, drive, and float.
It's got wings like a plane
And sails like a boat.
It can rocket through space.
It can dive in the sea.
It can dig through the ground.
It can climb up a tree.
I've made a machine.
It's fast and it's smart –
If only I knew
How to get it to start!

Richard James

15

Kitchen Sounds

Porridge gloops
A sausage sizzles
The toaster clangs
The kettle whistles
Washing spins
People chatter
Knives chop
Dishes clatter
Taps gush
Pans clink
Water gurgles
In the sink.

The light clicks off.
Night-time comes
And in the dark
The freezer hums.

Richard James

17

Mr Mad's Machine

Mr Mad has made a machine
To take you round the world.
Its wheels are square. Its tail is long.
Its wings are thin and curled.

It blows out rings of purple smoke.
The engine squeaks and squeals.
The jets are very powerful.
They're made of cotton reels.

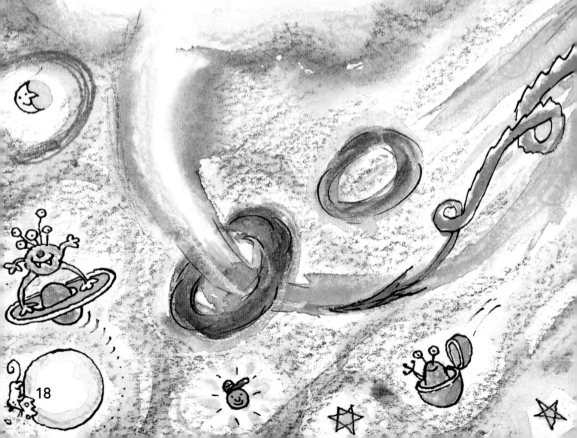

I wonder what it would be like
To fly in the machine.
It is the strangest sort of plane
That I have ever seen!

Tony Mitton

19

The Diggers

The diggers grab the soil up
in their mighty metal jaws.
They growl around the roadworks
like a herd of dinosaurs.
They look so much like monsters
with their rows of metal teeth,
tossing, digging, chomping
at the earth and rocks beneath.
They crunch and chew all day.
Their mighty engines roar.
They prowl around the roadworks
like a herd of dinosaurs.

Marian Swinger

The Double-Decker Bus

We like riding
on the double-decker bus.
Up on the top deck, that's the place for us.

In the front seat
with the driver down below,
We give the orders, tell him where to go.

We tell him when to speed up,
and when to slow down.
We drive the double-decker through the town.

We drive it up the hill
and park by the gate.
We make sure that the bus is never late.

We like riding
on the double-decker bus.
The front seat on the top deck –
That's the place for us!

John Foster

The Day the Hose Flipped

'Right,' said Dad,
'I'll turn the hose on
Round the back.'
We were washing the car –
It was really black.

We waited a bit
Me and our Chris,
Then the water came through
With a noisy hiss.

The water came through
With a splutter and a gush,
It came bursting through
With a mighty rush.

And the hose came alive
Like a twisting snake.
It soaked Chris's jeans
As if he'd jumped in the lake.

It drenched my dress.
The hose still flipped about,
And next door's cat
Got a waterspout.

When Dad arrived back,
He said, 'Gosh!
It's *the car* that's supposed
To be getting a wash!'

Eric Finney

Many Ways to Travel

There are many ways to travel
and one that I like
is to zoom down a hill
on a mountain bike.

There are many ways to travel
and another that's nice
is to slide on a sledge
on the snow and ice.

There are many ways to travel
and isn't it fun
to sail on the sea
in the wind and sun?

There are many ways to travel
but the best by far
is to ride on a rocket
to a distant star.

Tony Mitton

Two, One, Zero

Count down, count down,
Rocket leaving soon.
Count down, count down,
Leaving for the moon.

Count down, count down,
Minutes flicker by.
Count down, count down,
All eyes on the sky.

Count down to blast off,
Counting down from ten.
Count down to blast off,
For the rocket men.

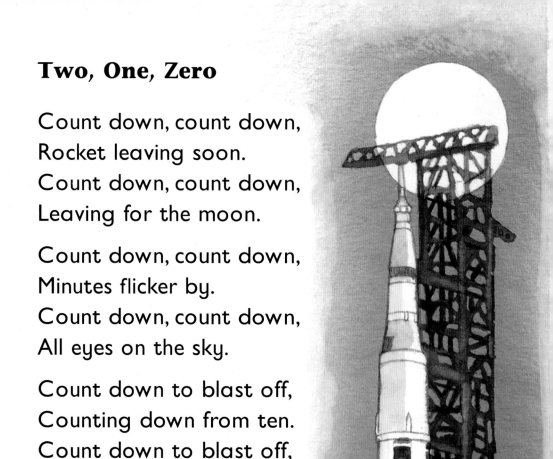

Blast off! Blast off!
Rocket in the air.
I'd like to be an astronaut,
Alone in space up there.

Barbara Ireson

Night Ride

When I can't sleep,
I shut my door
And sit on the rug
On my bedroom floor.

I open the window.
I close my eyes
And say magic words
Till my carpet flies.

Zooming over gardens,
Chasing after bats,
Hooting like an owl
And frightening the cats.

Then when I feel sleepy
And dreams are in my head,
I fly back through my window
And snuggle down in bed.

Celia Warren

33

Through the Dark

'We'll drive through the dark,' Dad said,
'And avoid the jams that way.'
So we set out well before midnight
At the start of our holiday.

Above us the big black sky
With a glimpse of a star or two.
In front of us, long weary hours
With nothing much to do.

Mum thought she spotted a fox
As we skirted the edge of a town,
I'm sure that I saw a UFO
With its ray of light beaming down.

We stopped for something to eat
At a twenty-four hour café,
Then hour after hour passed by
On our dark strip of motorway.

34

Till Dad said, 'It's really a shame,
You're missing a gorgeous sunrise.'
But I was too tired to notice;
I just couldn't open my eyes.

Brian Moses

Driving Along

Sometimes when I sit in my car,
In the driving seat,
I pretend that I am driving
Down a busy street.

I turn a corner carefully.
There are traffic lights ahead.
I put my foot down on the brake
Because they are turning red.

I steer past lots of other cars.
I overtake a bus.
I turn into a car park
and I find a place for us.

I go and buy the ticket.
I carefully lock the door.
Then, when Mum has done the shopping,
I drive her home once more.

John Foster

The Time Machine

Roll up, roll up, and on you climb,
I'll take you travelling back through time.
I'll show you things you've never seen.
All aboard my time machine!

Count down from ten. We're off so fast
That years and years are whizzing past.
We've stopped. Where are we? In a wood.
A man in green: it's Robin Hood!

And off again through history,
Let's stop in forty-five BC.
Look! Romans marching to and fro.
They don't look friendly. Time to go.

And further back and further back
We land now on a forest track.
No human footprints on the ground.
No people yet, so what's that sound?

39

A crash, a grunt, a groan, a roar –
Look out! A long-lost dinosaur!
Quick, back on board, count down from ten –
Phew! Just in time, we're home again.

Richard James

A Bucketful of Spells

Play the rhyming game **Can a goat float?** *Take it in turns to think of an animal and together add a rhyming word which asks what the animal can do, e.g. Can a dog jog? Can a kangaroo chew? In some cases, you may be able to suggest several alternatives, e.g. Can an owl scowl? Can an owl howl? Can an owl prowl? Can an owl foul?*

Ten Things Found in a Wizard's Pocket

Ian McMillan

1. A dark night.

*Aixpqoppxyfixzorapbbbies
Efkopolotooronqzypotopol
Zzzopotomangroututzoipneepto*

2. Some words that nobody could ever spell.

3. A glass of water full to the top.

5. A vest made from spider's webs.

4. A large elephant.

10. A snoring rabbit.

9. A bag of magic mints you can suck forever.

8. A bucket full of stars and planets, to mix with the dark night.

7. A bill from the Wand Shop.

Magic Dust .10p
Star Glitter .20p
Rainbow Light .30p
Silver Mist .50p
Total 110p

6. A handkerchief the size of a car park.

Just Practising

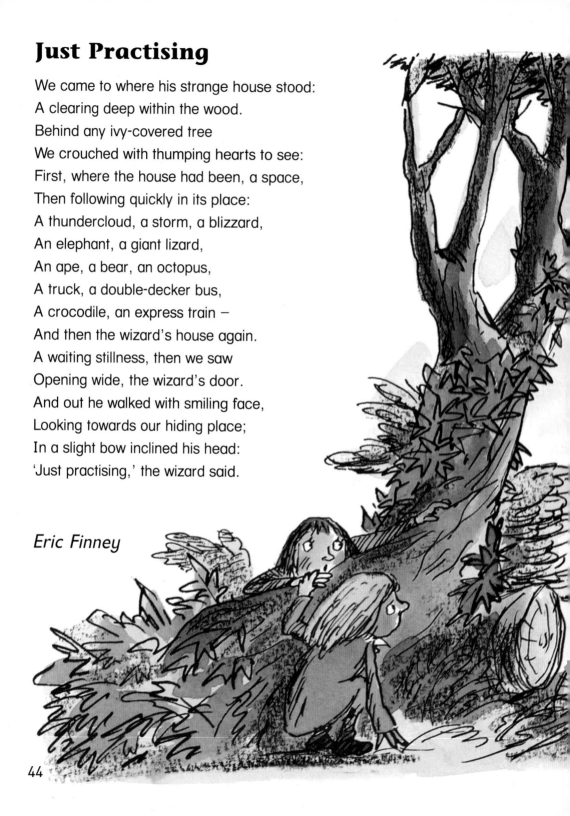

We came to where his strange house stood:
A clearing deep within the wood.
Behind any ivy-covered tree
We crouched with thumping hearts to see:
First, where the house had been, a space,
Then following quickly in its place:
A thundercloud, a storm, a blizzard,
An elephant, a giant lizard,
An ape, a bear, an octopus,
A truck, a double-decker bus,
A crocodile, an express train –
And then the wizard's house again.
A waiting stillness, then we saw
Opening wide, the wizard's door.
And out he walked with smiling face,
Looking towards our hiding place;
In a slight bow inclined his head:
'Just practising,' the wizard said.

Eric Finney

45

Wizard

Under my bed I keep a box
With seven locks,

And all the things I have to hide
Are safe inside:

My rings, my wand, my hat, my shells,
My book of spells.

I could fit a mountain into a shoe
If I wanted to,

Or put the sea in a paper cup
And drink it up.

I could change a cushion into a bird
With a magic word,

Or turn December into spring,
Or make stones sing.

I could clap my hands and watch the moon,
Like a white balloon,

Come floating to my windowsill ...

One day I will.

Richard Edwards

Meddling Muddle

'Don't touch that Magic Spell Book!'
The wizard warned the boy.
'Just get on with the sweeping,
I'm off to see King Roy.'

The wizard left the workshop.
The boy rushed up the stair.
He rummaged through the bookcase
And found the spellbook there.

He turned the pages quickly
To find the Brushing Spell.
He chanted all the verses.
He thought that all was well.

And then he started shrinking!
He got a dreadful fright.
He'd cast the spell so quickly
He hadn't said it right.

The wizard came back later.
He peered around the door.
The boy had disappeared.
A mouse was on the floor.

'You foolish little creature!
You've meddled with my book.
I'll have to turn you back again.
Now. Let me take a look.'

He pulled his cloak around him
And counted up to ten.
There was a bolt of lightning!
The boy stood there again.

'Now let that be a lesson.'
The wizard's voice was cold.
'NEVER play with magic,
And do as you are told!'

Wendy Larmont

Magic Man

The Magic Man in his magic suit
Plays a magic tune on his magic flute.
From his magic pocket plucks a magic cat
Pulls a magic rabbit from his magic hat.

His magic fingers
Make cards disappear,
Pull golden coins
From his magic ear.

When I grow older, if I can,
I'll learn to be a Magic Man.

John Kitching

Sailing Past the Planets

Type or write out poems for your child to illustrate and together make a book of favourite poems. Encourage your child to think of a title and to make it like a real book with a cover, a title page and a contents list.

Space

Space is . . .

      Planets like Pluto, Jupiter, and Mars,
      The Milky Way and billions of stars,
      Rockets, spaceships, UFOs,
      Mean, ugly creatures with 36 toes.
      Black holes, moons, and solar rays,
      Dark cold places without any days,
      Robots, space stations, laser guns,
      Different galaxies with different suns.

Space is a place I'd love to see
If hungry monsters won't eat me.

Robert Heidbreder

The Solar System Tour

Climb aboard! Yes, climb aboard!
You'll have a lifetime's thrill!
You'll love the Solar System tour.
We know, we *know* you will!

We'll whizz you right round Saturn,
then Mercury, then Mars!
See Venus, and see Neptune!
You'll spot six million stars!

Jupiter and Uranus!
Pluto! Our Earth and Moon!
So, climb aboard the spaceship!
Be quick! We're leaving soon!

Wes Magee

Journey Into Space

We went on a journey
A journey, a journey.
We went in a rocket
Jaswinder and me.
We went past the moon
And we went past the planets.
We sailed into Sunspace,
Jaswinder and me.
We landed at daybreak
At daybreak, at daybreak,
We landed in secret,
Jaswinder and me.
Then the aliens found us
And danced all around us
And made plans to crown us
Jaswinder and me.
But we climbed in our rocket,
Our rocket, our rocket,
And zoomed back to earth,
Just in time for our tea.

Irene Yates

Moonbase Classroom Three

This is Moonbase classroom three
and we're spending Christmas in Space,
We never thought we'd finish in time,
it's really been quite a race.

We've made an effort for Christmas;
strung paper chains from the stars,
while Santa Claus in full space gear
is steering a course for Mars.

We think this must be the first time
anyone's partied on the moon.
'What about weightlessness?' we ask,
'Would jelly stay on the spoon?'

Our teacher says, after the holiday
we'll be starting on something new,
but robots and moonshots are much more fun
than anything else we might do.

It's seldom that something we've done at school
has given us all such a thrill,
we've really been over the moon,
this term has been better than brill!

Brian Moses

Spaceship Race

Look, look,
it's the spaceship race –
Mars to Jupiter.
What a pace!
Rockets whizzing
all over the place.

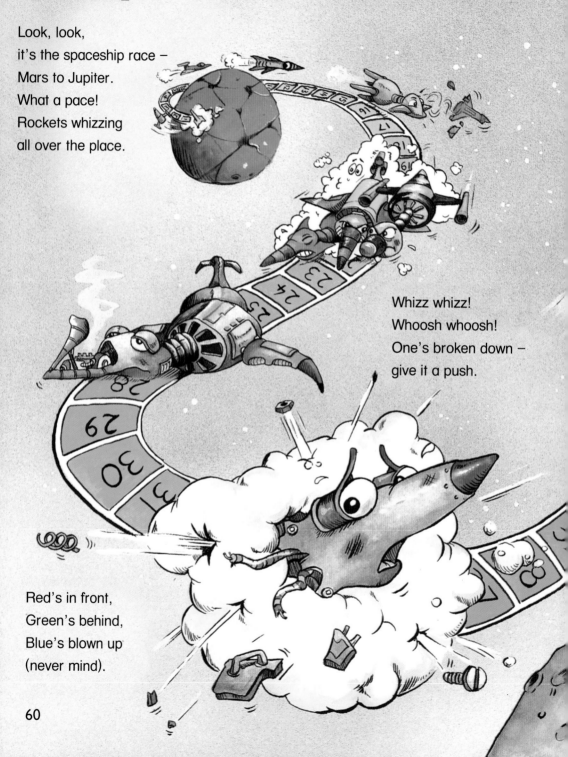

Whizz whizz!
Whoosh whoosh!
One's broken down –
give it a push.

Red's in front,
Green's behind,
Blue's blown up
(never mind).

Yellow goes faster,
Green's overtaken,
Green's going to win
if I'm not mistaken.

Green's going to win –
I bet you my dinner.
Green's going to
. . . oh no!
Red is the winner.

Charles Thomson

The Flying Reptiles Race

Five flying reptiles were just about to dine.
The dinner had arrived and it looked just fine.
Then up jumped a bossy one and shouted with glee,
'I bet that I could beat you to the Far-Away Tree!'

The other reptiles laughed and they cried, 'No way!
We're the fastest in the land, we could beat you any day!'
The bossy one boasted, 'I am the fastest one!'
But they all disagreed. So the race was on.

They lined up on the cliff edge ready to begin.
Five flying reptiles each saying, 'I'll win!'
They gazed across the ocean stretching far beyond the sand.
'The winner,' said the bossy one, 'is first back to land.'

Then 'Go!' screeched the bossy one giving them a fright –
and four foolish reptiles flew off into the night.
One bossy greedy reptile went off alone to dine,
'They won't be back till dawn,' he said, 'the dinner is all mine!'

Irene Yates

Space Message

A spaceman
flew down from his distant kingdom
bringing a message
from one of the stars.

He stood in the street
in his garment of silver;
he shone on the houses,
he shone on the cars.

He shone in the faces of people
who listened;
they all closed their eyes,
but they heard what he said.

'Take care of your earth,
look after its creatures.
Don't leave your children
a planet that's dead!'

Irene Rawnsley

67

On a Starry Night

On a starry night
The stars twinkle
Like thousands of bright eyes
Watching us and winking.

On a cloudy night
The stars are hidden
As if someone
Has blindfolded them.

John Foster

From a Space Rocket

We looked back at the World
    rolling through Space
like a giant Moon with a calm
    cool silver face.

All its cities and countries
    had faded from sight;
all its mountains and oceans were turned
    into pure light.

Slowly, its noise and troubles
    all seemed to cease,
and the whole World was beauty and silence
    and endless peace.

Raymond Wilson

Crashing Through the Ceiling

*Look out for the **calligram** on page 81 and discuss how the words look like what they describe. Then try creating your own **calligram** together.*

Instructions for Giants

Please do not step on the climbing frame
Or drink up the swimming pools.
Try not to tread on the teachers
But please flatten all the schools.

Please do not block out the sunshine.
Please do not lean on the trees.
Please push all the rain clouds away,
But please, oh please, do not sneeze!

Please duck your head when jets fly by.
Please sew up the ozone layer.
Please mind where you're putting your great big feet
Please do not tread on that chair!

John Rice and John Foster

73

Giant Tale

He was . . .

As wide as an oak tree,
tall as a willow;
his snore was the thunder,
a mountain his pillow.

Each step brought an earthquake,
each breath blew a gale;
one laugh moved an ocean,
each tear filled a pail.

His mouth was a crater,
with snakes for a tongue;
his eyes were the size
of the earth and the sun.

One toe was as heavy
as Venus and Mars;
his forehead was Saturn,
his hair shone with stars.

Judith Nicholls

The Giant Visitor

Great big foot came
crashing through the ceiling,
stood heel to toe
on the settee;
great big stocking,
torn about the ankle,
great big leg,
a hairy knee.

Great big voice
came booming down the chimney;
'Yoo-hoo!
Is anybody there?
It's four o'clock,
I'm hungry,
so empty all your cupboards!
Cook a great big meal;

I WANT MY TEA!'

Irene Rawnsley

Fast Food Giant

Fast food for my giant, please,
Double-treble fries,
A fourteen-pounder in a bun,
A dozen hot fruit pies.

Fifty chicken nuggets, please.
How long will they take?
I'd better have a bucketful
Of mega-thick milkshake.

'Just a bag of doughnuts, please,
And a Monster Mac,'
He'll say with his gigantic grin –
'Delicious! When's lunch, Jack?'

Sue Cowling

QUEUE
HERE

79

The Great Water Giant

The Great Water Giant
has finished his bath.

He pulls the huge plug
out of the clouds.
He roars his thunderous laugh,
and a wet, slippery waterfall
spills out of a squelchy sky.

'Look out below,' he seems to shout,
as the water

```
s           p           g
p           l           u
l     s     i     p     s     s
o     p     s     l     h     l
o     l     h     o     e     u
s     a     e     s     s     s
h     s     s     h           s
e     h           e           e
s     e           s           s
      s
```

and soaks deep into the thirsty earth.

Ian Souter

Ogre

Down by the railway cutting
where the blackberries belong
they say there lives an ogre
twenty metres long.

He sleeps between the irons
that mark the broken track,
with worms and snails and foxgloves
and a girder by his back.

Thomas was picking berries.
He put them in a jar,
when a voice as loud as thunder
roared, 'Who do you think YOU are?'

Tom ran like a greyhound
with fear inside his head!
'That's certainly an ogre
who beats up boys for bread!'

He turned, turned at the corner,
safely reached his door . . . .
His mum said, 'What's the hurry?
What are you running for?'

Thomas, he tried to tell her . . . .
Thomas, he tried and tried,
but he couldn't say more than 'ogre' –
the words got stuck inside.

But Mum didn't stay to listen.
'You're dreaming, lad,' she said.
'Come on and eat your supper.
And after that, it's bed.'

Thomas tossed in his blanket.
He never closed an eye
until the last star faded
and morning broke the sky.

The early papers published
in letters white and black:
FOUND, A GIANT OGRE
DOWN BY THE RAILWAY TRACK!

Jean Kenward

85

The Sea

The sea can be angry.
The sea can be rough.
The sea can be wild.
The sea can be tough.

The sea can rip.
The sea can tear.
The sea can roar
Like a hungry bear.

The sea can be gentle.
The sea can be flat.
The sea can be calm
As a sleeping cat.

The sea can glide
Over the sand,
Stroking the beach
Like a giant hand.

John Foster

Everything's Giant

Everything's giant
when you're an ant.
There's a howling gale
when a dog starts to pant.

You push a boulder
(it's really a pea).
There's a buzzing plane
(it's just a bee).

Every human
is two miles high
(they cause an earthquake
when they walk by).

A blade of grass
is a mighty tree.
A puddle appears
to be the sea.

No one cares
when you puff and pant.
Everything's giant
when you're an ant.

Charles Thomson

All Giants

'I am a giant,' said the ant.
His friends laughed one and all.
'You're crazy,' murmured Butterfly,
And the bee said, 'Ant, you're small.'

'It all depends,' Ant stoutly said,
'On who's compared with me.
I repeat: I am a giant –
to this microbe on my knee.'

After a little thought his friends
Said, 'Ant, that's true.
It's as you say: It all depends.
So we're all giants too!'

Eric Finney

Giant Griff

Giant Griff
Sits on the cliff
With his legs dangling over the side.

The children stand
In a queue on the sand
To use his big toe as a slide.

John Foster

Glossary

calligram a word or piece of text that looks like what it is describing

couplet a pair of lines ending with words that rhyme

emphasise to put stress on a word or words

intonation varying the pitch of your voice, making it rise or fall in order to convey emotion or meaning

narrative in a style that tells a story

narrator the person or character who is telling a story

onomatopoeia the use of a word or phrase which has a sound that echoes its meaning, e.g. hiss, buzz, clatter

pattern a sequence of words or phrases that is repeated several times in a poem

rhyme words which end with the same sound or sounds are said to make a rhyme

rhyme scheme the pattern of rhymes in a poem

rhythm the flow of words or phrases in a poem, based on the number and type of syllables they have

theme the subject of a poem, or an idea such as friendship or celebration which runs throughout the poem

tone the way of varying your voice in order to convey emotion, feeling and meaning

verse a section of a poem, often with the same rhyme scheme as other sections

Index of First Lines